USER FRIENDLY
RESOURCES
EDUCATIONAL
PUBLISHERS
www.userfr.com

W0007839

Setting your Sights

Techniques for Learning to Learn

BOOK B: Building the Framework

Michael Gifford

© Published by User Friendly Resource Enterprises Ltd. Book No. 452B

TITLE:
Book Name: Setting Your Sights: techniques for learning to learn
Book Number: 452B
ISBN Number: 1-86968-240-8
Published: 2006

AUTHOR: Michael Gifford

ACKNOWLEDGEMENTS:
Editor: Paula Wagemaker
Designer: Graphic Solutions
Illustrations: Geraldine Sloane

PUBLISHER:
User Friendly Resources

United Kingdom Office	**New Zealand Office**	**Australian Office**
c/- AFM Ltd	PO Box 1820	PO Box 914
Units 8,9,10, Parkside	Christchurch	Mascot, NSW 2020
Laughton	Ph: 0508-500-393	Ph: 1800-553-890
Shortgate Lane	Fax: 0508-500-399	Fax: 1800-553-891
East Sussex BN8 6DG		
Ph: 0845-450-7502		
Fax: 0845-450-7501		

WEBSITE:
www.userfr.com

E-MAIL:
info@userfr.com

COPYING NOTICE

This is a photocopiable book and permission is given to schools or teachers who buy this resource to make photocopies or transparencies of all pages. The copies must be for internal school use only, and may not be given or sold to other educational institutions or teachers from other institutions.

COPYRIGHT

© User Friendly Resources 2006.

User Friendly Resources specialises in publishing educational resources for teachers and students across a wide range of curriculum areas, at early childhood, primary and secondary levels.

If you wish to know more about our resources, or if you think your resource ideas have publishing potential, please contact us at one of the above addresses.

Contents

©User Friendly Resource Enterprises. Copying permitted for purchasing school only.

The Brain: Your Magic Motor

Many of the skills described, and techniques suggested, in this book are to assist you to find what best suits your brain and your method of learning. Be an adventurer—experiment, practise and enjoy finding new ways of learning. Although there are some incredibly complex and advanced computers available today, your brain is far superior to any of them. The brain is your most precious possession, and you need to know how to use and care for it. There are a number of excellent books on the brain you will enjoy reading. This chapter is just an introduction to some of its interesting features.

Activity 1 Brain Care—Why It's Important

- How well do you look after your brain? Read the following text, answering the questions, and at the end of it discuss in groups or with a friend what changes you could make in your life to keep your brain fit and healthy.

The Basic Facts

Weight: 1.5. kilos—a tiny percentage of your body weight.
Size: Similar to a small grapefruit.

Nourishment of the Brain

Water: The essential nourishment.
Oxygen: 20% of the body's oxygen intake is needed by the brain.
Food: A balanced diet—the 5+ a day routine is ideal brain food.

Some Implications

1. You cannot do better than to drink water. Up to 8 glasses a day will be the boost needed to keep you and your brain active and in good condition.

   - How much water do you drink each day?
   Develop the habit of having a glass of water on your desk as you study.

2. In societies where mothers are undernourished, children may develop up to 50% fewer brain cells, and that part of the brain responsible for limb co-ordination may be impaired.

   - Do you have a balanced diet or are junk foods the norm?
   Develop the habit of snacking on fresh fruit or vegetables.

©User Friendly Resource Enterprises. Copying permitted for purchasing school only.

Setting Your Sights

3. A baby born to a mother who smokes may subsequently show a lesser reading ability than a baby born to a non-smoking mother. This is because the foetus of a mother who smokes receives less oxygen than normal. And smoking fathers can be a danger. In 1995, a father was banned by a judge from smoking in his home when his young children came to visit him. His ex-wife was concerned that his heavy smoking was having a detrimental effect on the health of the children, particularly as one was asthmatic.

- Do you smoke? If so, have you considered the implications for your future children?
  Develop the no-smoking habit in yourself and your friends.

BELIEVE IT OR NOT?

Scientists have estimated that:

- The complexity of the entire network of the world's telephone systems is equivalent to a part of the brain the size of a normal garden pea.
- Up to a million chemical reactions take place in your brain at any particular moment.

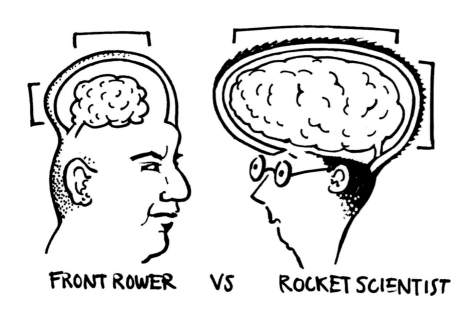

FRONT ROWER   VS   ROCKET SCIENTIST

©User Friendly Resource Enterprises. Copying permitted for purchasing school only.

Activity 2 The Triune Brain

- Did you know that your brain is made up of three parts–the reptilian, the limbic and the neo-cortex? Together, these three parts are known as the Triune Brain. As you read through the following descriptions of each part, work through the associated activities, all the time thinking about the implications of the different brain parts for how you learn and study. Check out your answers and ideas with your friends or family.   Do they agree with the picture you've developed of your learning and study habits?

Reptilian (Primitive) Brain

This part of the brain gives animals their sense of territory and physical space. It is responsible for your instincts and your basic survival and self-defence mechanisms. So when you put your hand on a hot element, the Reptilian Brain acts immediately and your instinct demands—withdraw! There is no logical process involved. You do not think, "Now this element is red hot, it must be almost 200 degrees. Therefore my hand will burn badly if I leave it on the element." Common sense says, "Take it off!"

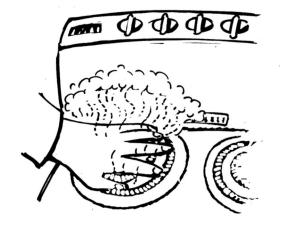

The Reptilian Brain likes **habits** and **rituals**— patterns that are repeated and result in the same expected outcome. Take my cat, for example. She knows that food time is a ritual, and when and where she will be fed each morning. We humans are the same. Our individual morning routines have become habit. It is said that it takes 30 days to develop an unshakeable **habit** or **ritual**. So use this new knowledge of your Reptilian Brain to develop **ritual** in your study.

Some examples:

- \# Study at set times.
- \# Study in the same place.
- \# Set yourself targets and goals.
- \# Keep to your study plan.

- Make a list of appropriate **rituals** you can develop into **habits** so as to make your study more effective.

©User Friendly Resource Enterprises. Copying permitted for purchasing school only.

Setting Your Sights

Limbic (Middle) Brain

This part of the brain is concerned with social interactions and your health, immune and hormone systems. It is the Limbic part of the brain that drives your sexual urges. Emotions are a key area of interest for the Limbic Brain, and any event that is strongly associated with **feelings** will remain embedded in your memory (your first 100 in cricket; your first kiss; the day you went white-water rafting; your first 'solo' drive; that magic visit to Mt. Maunganui; the school ball; eating Aunt Megan's pavlova at Christmas time; that great job interview at McDonald's).

Many older people (well, those alive in the '60s!) remember exactly where they were and what they were doing when they first heard of President John F. Kennedy's assassination. You probably can remember exactly what you were doing when you heard the news of the terrorist attacks on the World Trade Centre in New York.

- Ask your grandparents what they were doing the day President Kennedy died? What emotions did they feel when they heard the news.

Probably, they felt shock and horror, just as you may have done when hearing of the death of a famous person in tragic circumstances. While these emotions help set a memory, they are not the best emotions for effective learning. For this to occur, your emotions need to be *positive*. If you are emotionally drained or tired, or if you are bored, you will not learn, and your brain will move into Reptilian mode—where there is no memory. If your emotions make you over-excited and unable to focus, you'll again find learning difficult.

The Limbic Brain really controls your **state** and **attitude**. The more **positive** your feelings, the more you will learn.

- Using this new knowledge of your Limbic Brain, jot down at least three techniques that would give your learning a positive emotional basis.

Neo-Cortex (Thinking) Brain

The Neo-Cortex is the part of the brain that gives we humans our fantastic ability to **think, reason, talk, remember** and **write**.

It is the most amazing part of our brain and contains something like 10,000,000,000 brain cells. Just by way of comparison, the adult bee has about 7,000 of these brain cells (called neurons)—the number a human embryo grows in three seconds—but with these a bee can build a honeycomb, signal to a companion and calculate distances.

©User Friendly Resource Enterprises. Copying permitted for purchasing school only.

Each neuron looks a bit like a miniature octopus, or tree with scraggly branches. Each time something reaches one of your senses it creates a thought or impression that travels from the brain cell along the branches creating new connections.

It is not the number of brain cells you have that is important. What is crucial is the number of connections that develop between those brain cells.

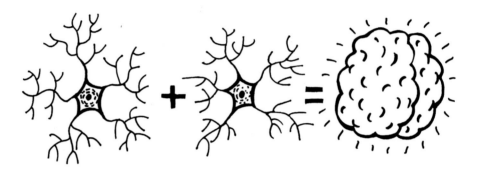

> *It is said that the brain of Albert Einstein, the world-famous physicist and mathematician, lies in a glass jar in a university in the USA. It is no bigger than average, but researchers say that its dark colouring is evidence of the large number of connections linking Einstein's brain cells.*

You literally expand your brain through use. It's been estimated that most of us use only about 4% of our brain capacity, so there's plenty of room to expand, and little chance of dying from over-use!

What's more, there's no evidence to suggest that the brain deteriorates with age. The challenge as we get older is to keep using our brains and exercising our minds by reading, enjoying hobbies, looking for new experiences, and by being vigorous and creative.

The motto is: USE IT OR LOSE IT.

> **Did You Know?**
>
> - **Winston Churchill** did not become Prime Minister of Britain until he was 66 years of age.
> - **Michelangelo**, the artist and sculptor, was still energetic and creative in his eighties.
> - In 1996, the English composer **Vivian Ellis** wrote three new songs for his musical **Listen to the Wind.** His age? 92.

©User Friendly Resource Enterprises. Copying permitted for purchasing school only.

Activity 3   Right Brain, Left Brain

- Read the following description about the right and left sides of the brain. Then draw the picture of the head below (picture only; not the words), looking at the lists either side of it.

    - What school subjects do you think are mainly right brain subjects, and which are left brain? Put down your ideas either side of the head.
    - What about occupations? Can you name occupations that require basic right brain skills and some that are mainly left brain? Again, use the head picture. You might want to use a different coloured pen.
    - Do you consider yourself to be predominantly a left or a right brain person? In other words, do you feel more comfortable with subjects involving logic and analysis, or with those that are more imaginative and artistic?

The Two Sides of the Brain

The Neo-Cortex is known to have two distinct sides, which can be regarded as two identical brains, working together and linked by a complex network of up to 300 million nerve fibres (the Corpus Callosum). The Corpus Callosum acts like a giant telephone exchange, switching messages from one side to the other.

One function of the **RIGHT BRAIN** is to control activities on the left side of the body. If this side of the brain is damaged the left side of the body may become paralysed.

One function of the **LEFT BRAIN** is to control activities on the right side of the body. If this side of the brain is damaged the right side of the body may become paralysed.

The **RIGHT BRAIN** controls several several specific mental activities:

The **LEFT BRAIN** controls very different mental activities:

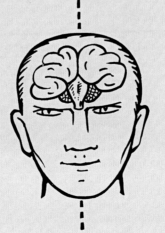

Right Brain	Left Brain
Rhythm	Numbers
Creativity	Rational Ideas
Pictures/Symbols	Sequence
Music Centre	Time Awareness
Colour	Logic
Imagination	Language
Day Dreaming	

©User Friendly Resource Enterprises. Copying permitted for purchasing school only.

Did You Know?

When you listen to a song, the **left brain** will basically be attending to the words, the **right brain** to the music.

Traditionally, most of our learning has been on **left brain** lines. So notes have tended to be written on successive horizontal lines—logically and in order. Only in recent times have students been encouraged to engage in **right brain** activities involving colour and imagination as they learn.

Many great thinkers have found that their greatest inspiration has come from **right brain** activities such as day dreaming. Einstein acknowledged that he discovered his famous Theory of Relativity while lounging on a hillside one sunny afternoon and not sitting at the desk in his office. How many of your "great thoughts" have come when you are relaxed—sitting in an easy chair, lounging on the bed, out fishing, in the shower?

One key to successful learning is to develop learning activities which utilise your whole brain— combining activities from your preferred side with those that need developing from the other.

Watch a young baby with a toy or even a piece of paper. The baby will look at it, poke it, tear at it, hit it, drop it, eat it, crunch it, examine it. The baby is learning, experimenting, checking—using both its analytical left brain and its creative right brain. We all need to explore and use our brains as young children do.

Leonardo da Vinci —the best painter, sculptor, architect, inventor and engineer of his or almost any other century. His skills were a real blending of left and right brain activities. He even used colour in his drawings and plans.

©User Friendly Resource Enterprises. Copying permitted for purchasing school only.

Activity 4   How Good Is Your Memory?

- Test your memory:

  1) Write down your, name, address, telephone number, date of birth.
  2) Write down the names of three friends and their telephone numbers.
  3) Draw a sketch of the layout of your home.
  4) Draw a map of the route you take to get to school.
  5) Write down the subject you have Period 5 on Mondays (or Day 1).
  6) Write down the names of three famous film stars.

- How many of these tasks did you find difficult?

The point is: There is no such thing as a bad memory. In the activity above you've just proved how good your memory really is.

Most of us are a bit like the boy who comes home with FAIL all over his school report. His father is furious and says, "Andy, that's it—no more rugby until you get your grades up—and that starts from tomorrow!"

"But gee, Dad, I can't miss the England – Australia rugby game! It's the best. I'll never forget the 2003 World Cup Final. Robinson's try in the first half, Jonny Wilkinson's drop goal to win the game, and Martin Johnson holding up the trophy."

Andy's memory is fine. Maybe his attitude to school is wrong, or maybe he just doesn't know how to study— to set goals, to plan, to use his skills, and to develop his study techniques.

- How well can you relate to Andy? Do you find that there are situations where your memory is just fine, and others where you have trouble? In each instance, try to think about the things that are helping or hindering your memory.

11

©User Friendly Resource Enterprises. Copying permitted for purchasing school only.

Activity 5 Memory Quizzes

• In your class or with your friends or family, try out the quizzes at the end of this book (page 55). **DON'T** look at the quizzes now, but choose someone to act as "quizmaster", and get him or her to follow the instructions at the start of each quiz. At the end of each quiz (**NOT** before), see if the results tally with what's written below and check out the implications for your learning.

Quiz One: What the Results Show

When the quiz is taken by a group, the results always show the same trend. Most of you will remember lines from the beginning of the song and from the end, but probably have difficulty with the words in the middle. In other words, you remember best what you heard **first** and what you heard **last**.

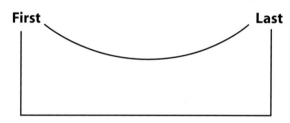

IMPLICATIONS FOR LEARNING

It is important to **study with breaks**—check back to Activity 13 in Book A This will give you opportunities to have plenty of **firsts** and **lasts** as you study.

Quiz Two: What the Results Show

As with Quiz No 1, most people will remember words from the beginning of the list (**first)** and from the end (**last)**. Many will also remember the group of words at the end for another reason—they are **linked** through the common letter '**f**' and also through 'fresh' and 'fish'. The word 'and' is usually remembered because it is repeated several times, and 'Shortland St'and 'Queen Elizabeth' will always feature because they are **different**, can be **visualised** and they **stand out**.

©User Friendly Resource Enterprises. Copying permitted for purchasing school only.

Setting Your Sights

A graph of the results from an average group of people would look like this.

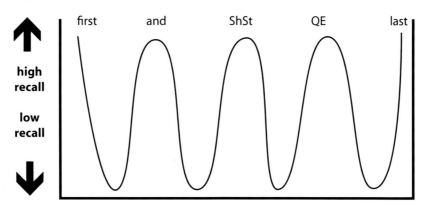

IMPLICATIONS FOR LEARNING

Key words

REPETITION	LINKING	OUTSTANDING

• The more you go over material the better it will stick.
 	
• Go over the day's work each night.
 	
• Then check again after a day. **Colin Rose** advocates using the 10-48-7 technique. Check your knowledge after:
   10 minutes
   48 hours
   7 days.
 	
• A skill or knowledge is remembered if **USED** within 24 hours.
	• Look for patterns
	
	• Go from information you **KNOW** and link to that you **DON'T KNOW**. For example, how do you describe a **ZEBRA** to someone who has never seen on? You say it is like a **HORSE** with black and white stripes.
	
	• Look for logical **LINKS** between ideas.
	e.g. In shipping terms, **PORT** is on the **LEFT** (both are four letter words) The **PORT** side light is **RED** (Port is a Red Wine).
		• You remember real things more easily than abstract ideas.
		
		• Create a picture or a story.
		
		• Make images memorable and unique.
		
		• Use your 5 senses in work—sight, sound, taste, smell, touch.

©User Friendly Resource Enterprises. Copying permitted for purchasing school only.

13

- Look at the drawing below. It illustrates the importance of **repetition** in the memory process. We can all remember an item for a short time (such as a telephone number) but repetition is the key to **Long-Term Memory**.

1) Write down 3 meaningful link or cue words to go with the word **BEACH**.

e.g. BEACH: sand	Bondi	surf
e.g. BEACH: holiday	sandcastle	sea

Researchers have found that given a list of 20 words, those who were able to refer to a set of **link** words or **cues** remembered up to 90% of the words on the list, even weeks later. Participants who did not use this technique scored far lower.

2) Now look at the list of 20 words below. Use about 20 seconds on each word and write down 3 personal **cues** for each. When you have completed the list, put it aside.

computer	wallet
roof	fantastic
Lincoln	headache
Turkey	Christmas tree
calendar	doctor
spade	choir
blankets	koala
Harbour Bridge	butterfly
bamboo	fear
drums	kauri

3) Later, look at the cues **only** and write down as many of the words on the list above as you can. You will be surprised at how many of the original words are remembered through their **link** words or **cues**.

4) Repeat the exercise after a week, and check your results. This will indicate how strong your cue words are, and how good your memory actually is.

14

©User Friendly Resource Enterprises. Copying permitted for purchasing school only.

Activity 6 Memory Methods

Visualisation

- Try one or all of following visualisations.

  1) You're a waiter or waitress who has to learn the 'Specials' for the day—in two minutes. Look at the following list, and picture each item in your mind. Visualise and exaggerate them. Make your images of them **outstanding** and **link** them in some way if you can. Then put away the list, let your mind recall the images and either write down the "Specials" or tell them to a friend or parent.

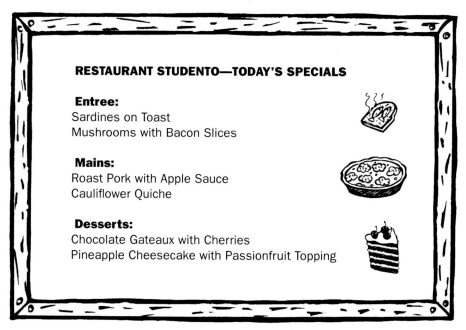

RESTAURANT STUDENTO—TODAY'S SPECIALS

Entree:
Sardines on Toast
Mushrooms with Bacon Slices

Mains:
Roast Pork with Apple Sauce
Cauliflower Quiche

Desserts:
Chocolate Gateaux with Cherries
Pineapple Cheesecake with Passionfruit Topping

2) Take the names of the Seven Dwarfs. To remember them, turn them into a story you can easily visualise.

DOPEY   SLEEPY   GRUMPY   DOC   HAPPY   BASHFUL   SNEEZY

3) Take a character in a novel or play you are studying. As you read, pause from time to time to reflect and relive the events which have just been described to you. Imagine you actually **are** the character. Try to **visualise** the events and experience the feelings and reactions you would have to the different situations in the story.

©User Friendly Resource Enterprises. Copying permitted for purchasing school only.

Understanding

- Understanding is vital to all other memory work. Read aloud the following description of the rules of cricket. (We're assuming that the team is a male one!) You'll get no idea of what the game is about from these rules unless you already understand the game. Then, it actually does make sense.

THE RULES OF CRICKET
(as explained to a foreign visitor)

You have two sides–one out in the field and one in.

Each man that's in the side that's in goes out, and when he's out he comes in and the next man goes in until he's out.

When they are all out, the side that's out comes in and the side that's been in goes out and tries to get those coming in out.

Sometimes you get men still in and not out.

When both sides have been in and out, including the not outs

that's the end of the game!

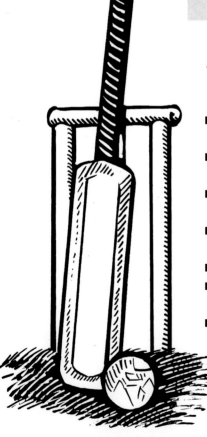

- Try these other techniques to help develop your **UNDERSTANDING**.

- Develop an **overview** of a topic in order to follow the broad principles or outline before you try to memorize.
- Learn **principles**—this is easier than learning individual examples.
- Understand **meanings** of words and phrases—this is vital to your memory work.
- Understand **context**—it provides the "map" or overview of the material.
- Learn by **example**—this is better than learning by rote.
- **Explain** the material to someone else—this is one of the best ways of learning.
- **Ask** teachers, friends, or parents to explain an issue until you understand.

16

©User Friendly Resource Enterprises. Copying permitted for purchasing school only.

Setting Your Sights

Number-Shape/Number-Rhyme (Two-Memory Systems)

A number of memory experts advocate the Number-Shape or the Number-Rhyme methods of learning. These visualisation and linking techniques are particularly useful when memorising lists. Usually there is no "understanding" required in the learning.

The **NUMBER-SHAPE** system links the numbers 1 to 10 to objects which have the same shape as the numbers. To memorise the list, you link what you want to remember to the image shape of your system. Your own drawing of each item in the list below can then be **linked visually** to each item you wish to remember. If the first item to remember is the "Mona Lisa", then imagine a large pencil drawing a black moustache on the perfect face of this famous painting.

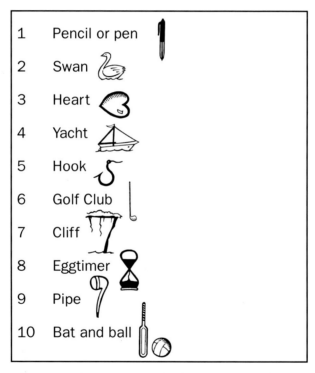

1	Pencil or pen
2	Swan
3	Heart
4	Yacht
5	Hook
6	Golf Club
7	Cliff
8	Eggtimer
9	Pipe
10	Bat and ball

- Using the **NUMBER–SHAPE** technique, learn this list of words in the correct order. To memorise the following list, you may wish to draw each word as you go, or you can visualise a picture of each one in your head. For example, visualise a large PEN drawing a gum tree.

1.	Gum Tree	2.	Silk
3.	Chicken	4.	Highlighter
5.	Sock	6.	Window
7.	Train	8.	Calculator
9.	Book	10.	Calendar

©User Friendly Resource Enterprises. Copying permitted for purchasing school only.

The **NUMBER- RHYME** technique links the number to objects which **rhyme** with the number. It's a similar technique to that in the children's song "This Old Man".

1. Bun
2. Shoe
3. Tree
4. Door
5. Hive
6. Sticks
7. Heaven
8. Skate
9. Vine
10. Hen

- Using the **NUMBER-RHYME** technique, learn this list of words. Imagine that you are writing an essay on nuclear testing. You need to remember these words as your starters for the essay.

1.	France	2.	Pacific Islands
3.	Greenpeace	4.	Protest flotilla
5.	Protests	6.	12 miles exclusion zone
7.	110 kilotonnes	8.	World condemnation
9.	Trade	10.	World court

©User Friendly Resource Enterprises. Copying permitted for purchasing school only.

Activity 7 Memory Techniques Checklist

- Pin the following list of points up on your study noticeboard.

1) Study with **BREAKS**—to get many **FIRSTS** and **LASTS** into your learning.

2) Develop ways of **LINKING** information—use **CUES**.

3) Use **REPETITION**—one of the keys to memory. Or to put it another way, **REPEAT**, **REVISE**, **REHEARSE**.

4) Use all the senses to create unusual, **OUTSTANDING**, bizarre visual images.

5) Use as many different ways of learning as you can—and use them together for maximum effect. **Colin Rose**, an English writer who is recognised for his research into accelerated learning methods, puts it this way:

   We remember:

   20% of what we **READ**

   30% of what we **SEE**

   40% of what we **HEAR**

   50% of what we **SAY**

   60% of what we **DO**

   90% of what we **SEE, HEAR, SAY & DO**

   The more we can **combine** these factors in our learning, the more effective our learning will be.

6) Aim to **UNDERSTAND**, rather than rote learn without understanding.

©User Friendly Resource Enterprises. Copying permitted for purchasing school only.

Learning Styles

Activity 8 What Suits You Best?

- Look at the following comments from students. They're about the types of elements and conditions that students say affect their ability to learn. Which ones apply to you? What other ones could you add to develop a picture of the conditions under which you like to study?

"I just can't seem to work late at night."

"I never wake up properly until lunchtime."

I get restless sitting at a desk all the time."

"I like sitting in a firm-backed chair."

"I like to work in complete silence."

"Silence makes me nervous."

"I have a really bright light on my desk when I study."

"Fluorescent lights make me twitchy."

- Now read the text and accompanying list of study conditions on the following pages. When you've done that check out your preferences for each element on the following lines. Some of you may have no real preference one way or the other for some of these items. But if you do, use this knowledge when planning and organising your study.

ELEMENT	LOW	MEDIUM	HIGH
Sound	....		
Temperature	....		
Light	....		
Seating	....		
Structure	....		
Persistence	....		
Working alone	....		
Group work	....		
Intake	....		
Mobility	....		
Time of day	Morning	Afternoon	Evening
	....		

©User Friendly Resource Enterprises. Copying permitted for purchasing school only.

Setting Your Sights

LEARNING STYLES

The conditions under which a person studies and learns new material is the basis of learning style. Research has shown that people do learn in different ways. The American researchers, **Rita** and **Kenneth Dunn**, have highlighted a number of elements and conditions that can affect our learning. These are:

1) Sound

Some students work best in silence; others prefer quiet background music, sounds of nature, or busy working noises when they are engaged in a task.

If you respond to **music**, soft **baroque** music has been found to stimulate the mind and at the same time to provide a learning environment. Music with a steady rhythm of 60 beats per minute is ideal. Try working with soft baroque music in the background, and read a book such as **Colin Rose's "Accelerated Learning"** on the subject.

What is **not appropriate** is listening to loud heavy metal or rock music, and specially songs with words. These are a definite **distraction**. You will find yourself mouthing the words or tapping to the rhythm of the songs (which is fine at a concert) but a real **disaster** when learning. The mind cannot concentrate on two things at once.

- Try holding a conversation with someone and at the same time listen to what another person is saying on the telephone. It just can't be done. Your mind switches from one to the other. This is exactly what will happen if you try to study and listen to pop or rock music at the same time as you study.

2) Time of Day

Each of us has a best time at which to tackle mental tasks such as writing a letter, practising the piano or studying for a test. An activity that seems impossible at 8.00 a.m. for some may be easy at 4.00 p.m. Because our body systems vary, we all have our peaks and valleys at different times. So it is important to know when you're 'hot' and when you're not.

©User Friendly Resource Enterprises. Copying permitted for purchasing school only.

3) Temperature

Some people learn and study best in cool temperatures—so they should not study in hot, stuffy conditions. Others, who need warmth, should put on extra clothing. Studying in front of heaters or the fire is not good; neither is studying in the hot sun.

4) Light

Some students need brightly-lit study areas, while others are more efficient when the light is dimmer. Whatever the intensity of the light, it has been found that many people react badly to fluorescent lighting. If you find that these lights cause you problems, you are not alone, and you should try to find an alternative lighting source.

5) Seating

It has been estimated that up to 40% of students study more effectively when their seating is informal rather than the "normal" desk and chair arrangement. Libraries now cater for the informal learner by providing cushions and bean bags. Boys, in particular, often get restless in formal seating situations. They squirm, sit on their ankles, and even fall off their chairs trying to get comfortable.

6) Structure

Some people like assignments to be fully structured—with an exact title, the number of words specified, guidelines given on marking criteria (does spelling count? do I need to put references?), and so on. Others prefer assignments to be unstructured and open-ended, with general rather than specific directions. They like to be able to interpret and write without restrictions.

7) Persistence

Students with high persistence are those who feel compelled to complete a project once they have started it, and who will begin a new project only after the first has been completed. Those with lower persistence may start with a burst of energy, but soon need a break and like to vary their activities.

©User Friendly Resource Enterprises. Copying permitted for purchasing school only.

8) Individual/Group Preference

Some people do their best thinking and studying alone. They find the presence of other people a distraction. On the other hand, there are those who like working in pairs or in groups, and who do their best work when they have the stimulus of other people working on, or thinking about, the same task.

9) Intake

Some students eat, drink, chew or bite objects as they concentrate. These people need regular glasses of water or snacks as they study. (Their pencils are often decorated with tooth marks!) Others can work quite happily for long periods of time without needing food or drink.

10) Mobility

When a person is seated on a hard chair, 75% of the body weight is supported by about 10 square centimetres of bone. This causes many students to experience stress and discomfort, and they have difficulty sitting still even for a short time. They have the urge to stretch or move at regular intervals. In a three-hour exam, such students need to develop special strategies for stretching so as not to cause disruption in the exam room. Others are more fortunate and are able to remain seated and comfortable for longer.

©User Friendly Resource Enterprises. Copying permitted for purchasing school only.

Activity 9 Your Multiple Intelligences

- When you think of intelligence in a person, what do you think of? Chances are it's IQ (Intelligence Quotient), which basically measures your mathematical and English skills. IQ tests give you an IQ score of 140 or 90 or whatever. And once you have this IQ you are stuck with it! At least in most people's minds.

However, **Howard Gardner**, the American educationalist, has carried out important research in which he explains that we all possess special intelligences not measured by normal IQ tests. All are equally important in the development of our abilities and personalities. Unlike IQ tests, which tend to label you forever, you can continue to develop your skills in these Multiple Intelligences.

- Read the descriptions of Gardner's different intelligences on the following pages, and then rate your abilities in each using Chart A below.   Use this knowledge of your strengths to develop useful learning techniques. On Chart B, set a target and mark a level that you can be confident of reaching in each intelligence by, say, the end of the year.

CHART A

	Linguistic	Math/ Logical	Visual	Physical	Musical	Intra Personal	Inter Personal
HIGH							
LOW							

CHART B

	Linguistic	Math/ Logical	Visual	Physical	Musical	Intra Personal	Inter Personal
HIGH							
LOW							

24

©User Friendly Resource Enterprises. Copying permitted for purchasing school only.

Setting Your Sights

1) Linguistic Intelligence

Those strong in this intelligence have a talent with language and the ability to write and talk well. They are good at explaining things, and enjoy plays, poetry, conversation, letter writing and word puzzles. *Occupations* followed by those with strong **Linguistic Intelligence** include writers, journalists, speechwriters, politicians and public relations managers. **Famous people** with Linguistic Intelligence include writers *Janet Frame* and *Colleen McCullough*, wartime Prime Minister **Winston Churchill** and sports commentator/speaker**s Jeremy Coney and Richie Benaud.**

2) Mathematical/Logical Intelligence

Those strong in this intelligence have skills in Maths, and like logical explanations for events and situations. They like to establish systems, look for patterns and relationships, and arrange tasks in orderly sequences. **Occupations** followed by those with strong **Mathematical/Logical Intelligence** include mathematicians, lawyers, accountants, scientists and engineers. **Famous people** with Mathematical/Logical Intelligence include physicist **Ernest Rutherford**, fictional sleuth **Sherlock Holmes** and computer whizz **David Gapes**.

3) Visual/Spatial/Intelligence

Those with a strong **Visual/Spatial Intelligence** have the ability to visualise how things will eventually look. They are good at map reading and navigating, driving, parking, planning gardens, and packing holiday luggage into cars. They are always very observant and remember things visually. **Occupations** of those with a good Visual/Spatial Intelligence include artists, sculptors, architects, chess professionals, navigators and stage set designers. **Famous people** with Visual/Spatial Intelligence include painter and sculptor **Michelangelo**, architect **Sir Christopher Wren** and war strategist **Napoleon Bonaparte**.

4) Musical Intelligence

Those with **Musical Intelligence** have the ability to interpret and create music, and to keep pitch and rhythm. They are good at remembering tunes, and moving in time to music. **Occupations** of those with Musical Intelligence include composers, conductors, singers, piano-tuners and music teachers. **Famous people** with Musical Intelligence include opera singers **Joan Sutherland** and **Kiri Te Kanawa**, and composers **Paul McCartney** and **A**ndrew Lloyd **Webber**.

©User Friendly Resource Enterprises. Copying permitted for purchasing school only.

5) Physical Intelligence

Those with strong **Physical Intelligence** have the ability to move and run well, dance, build or construct something. They like to deal with problems physically, hands on. They remember best what they have actually done themselves. **Occupations** taken on by those with strong Physical Intelligence include athletes, dancers, doctors, sports professionals, mechanics and inventors. **Famous people** with Physical Intelligence include squash champion **Susan Devoy**, swimmer **Dawn Fraser**, heart surgeon **David Barratt-Boyes** and ice skaters **Torvill** and **Dean**.

6) Interpersonal Intelligence

Those with strong **Interpersonal Intelligence** have the ability to communicate well and get on with people. They are good at listening, managing and working with others, helping people and teaching and training people. They enjoy committee work. **Occupations** of those with Interpersonal Intelligence include teachers, social workers, counsellors, personnel managers, religious leaders and sales reps. **Famous people** with **Interpersonal Intelligence** include Christian prophet **Jesus Christ** and TV personality **Oprah Winfrey**.

7) Intrapersonal Intelligence

Those with strong Intrapersonal Intelligence have the ability to involve themselves in quiet, objective thinking and analysis. They are good at creating goals, planning and understanding their own feelings and moods. They enjoy privacy and doing things independently. **Occupations** of those with Intrapersonal Intelligence include philosophers,novelists and counsellors. **Famous people** with Intrapersonal Intelligence include the Indian leader **Mahatma Gandhi**, Greek philosopher **Plato** and motivational writer **Stephen Covey**.

©User Friendly Resource Enterprises. Copying permitted for purchasing school only.

Setting Your Sights

Activity 10 V A K—Using Your Senses

- Just as we're all different in terms of intelligences, we're also different in the ways that we take in information through our senses. **Learning**, in fact, **involves your whole body**. Look at the picture below. What sort of learning do you feel most comfortable with?

Some learn best by **listening**—hearing explanations, listening to lectures.

Some learn best with their **heads**—by thinking, grasping concepts, learning by heart, remembering.

Some learn best by **seeing** things and visualising—once they have seen it in their mind's eye they can remember it.

> *35% of people are mainly **V**ISUAL learners (Visual/Spatial Intelligence)*
>
> *25% of people are mainly **A**UDITORY learners (Linguistic Intelligence)*
>
> *40% of people are mainly **K**INESTHETIC learners (Physical Intelligence)*

Some learn by **talking**. Things only make sense when they can put them into their own words, discuss them.

Some learn best when it **feels** right—when things make sense in terms of their culture and their experience.

Some people learn best by **doing**—using their bodies and involving themselves physically—in practical and manual skills.

Researchers have grouped these different ways of learning into three main categories, known as **VAK**—**V**ISUAL, **A**UDITORY and **K**INESTHETIC.

©User Friendly Resource Enterprises. Copying permitted for purchasing school only.

Characteristics of VAK Learners

VISUAL (look)	AUDITORY (listen)	KINESTHETIC (do and feel)
- doodle when talking on the phone. - speak quickly. - spell well. - remember what is seen. - memorise by visual association. - are not distracted by noise. - are strong, fast readers.	- talk to themselves. - prefer lectures to reading. - like talking more than writing. - are good mimics of tone, pitch, timbre. - speak in rhythmic patterns. - remember by what is heard. - like telling jokes.	- speak slowly - move around when thinking and learning. - gesture frequently when speaking. - find it hard to sit still. - remember by doing. - use a finger as a pointer when reading.

- Consider the chart below, adapted from **Accelerate Your Learning** (Colin Rose). Check which responses best represent your personal preferences. This will give you an idea of your strengths in the visual, auditory and kinesthetic modes.

WHEN YOU		VISUAL	AUDITORY	KINESTHETIC
Spell	Do you	Picture the word?	Say the word phonetically	Write the word down to check that it feels right?
Are with people	Do you	Forget names but remember faces?	Forget faces but remember names?	Remember activities rather than the people?
Contact people	Do you	Like to meet them face to face?	Like to use the telephone?	Like to meet and talk with them while walking?
Relax	Do you	Like to see things— TV and movies, read or paint?	Like listening to the radio—talking or music?	Like being active— playing sports, games, dancing?
Thank someone	Do you	Write them a note of appreciation?	Give them verbal thanks?	Give them a hug or a pat on the back?
Read	Do you	Like descriptive passages; stop to imagine scenes?	Enjoy dialogue and conversation; "hear" characters talk?	Read very little, and when you do, prefer stories with plenty of action?
Learn	Do you	Like to see demonstrations, diagrams, posters?	Like lectures, talks and verbal instructions?	Prefer direct involvement —learning by taking part in activities?
Speak	Do you	Talk slowly and dislike listening to others for too long?	Talk quickly and become impatient when waiting to talk?	Gesture a lot and use expressive movements?
Listen	Do you	Look mainly at a speaker's facial expression?	Listen to a speaker's tone of voice?	Watch a speaker's movements?

©User Friendly Resource Enterprises. Copying permitted for purchasing school only.

Setting Your Sights

- When you've done that, rate your VAK abilities on the following A - E scale. How can you improve your strengths in each?

	A	B	C	D	E

My **VISUAL** strength: ....

My **AUDITORY** strength: ....

My **KINESTHETIC** strength: ....

Although you may be stronger in either visual (seeing), or auditory (listening) or kinesthetic (doing and feeling) modes, you do have abilities in each of them. If you can combine all three modes in your learning, you will increase your ability to remember.

Note: As you work through the remaining sections of Books B and C of this resource, notice how the activities tie in with different styles of learning and types of intelligence.

29

©User Friendly Resource Enterprises. Copying permitted for purchasing school only.

Mindmapping

Activity 11   What is Mindmapping?

- Look at the following diagrams, called **Mindmaps**, drawn by two students. Brainstorm in class or with friends as to why you think they're called mindmaps and what their purpose is. When you've done this, see how your ideas tally with the description of mindmapping that follows the pictures.

a)   On Tropical Cyclones

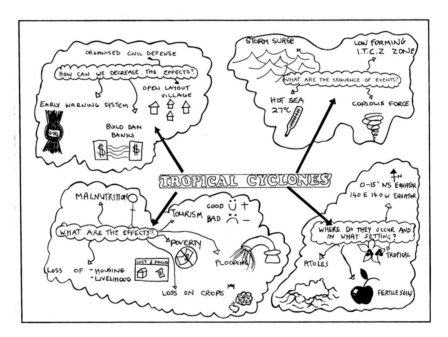

b)   On Crime and the Law

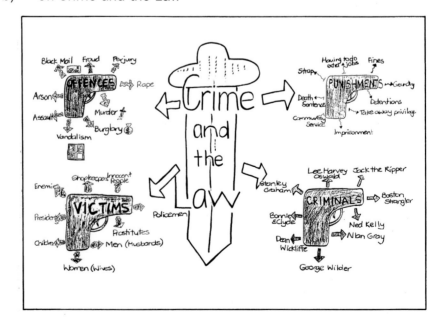

©User Friendly Resource Enterprises. Copying permitted for purchasing school only.

Setting Your Sights

> A **MINDMAP** is a **Visual, Colourful, Striking** summary of a topic that is **Memorable** and easily recalled.

The **Mindmapping** technique was coined and "invented" by the English researcher and writer Tony Buzan and further developed and refined by teachers and educationalists throughout the world.

Visual (**right brain**) learners find Mindmapping a particularly useful way of making notes. That's because when you take notes, writing on white paper, with letters the same size and with the same margins (rather like the pages in this book), you are following **left brain** guidelines, which is fine if you favour your left brain. But if not, you may find this traditional method sets you up for some boring and non-memorable notes.

MINDMAPS HAVE MANY ADVANTAGES:

- They are **personal** to you. Other people's words and diagrams are never so memorable as your own!

- They are **your** interpretations and **your** words.

- They:
  - Are fast to create
  - Are easy to visualise
  - Contain key ideas
  - Are compact—on one page
  - Show connections between ideas
  - Allow you to organise ideas
  - Allow you to add ideas
  - Are visually attractive

- You can **use** Mindmaps for:
  - Getting started—brainstorming
  - Planning a speech
  - Summarising notes and texts
  - Summarising articles and books
  - Summarising seminars and presentations
  - Planning assignments and essay questions
  - Planning exam answers
  - Solving problems
  - Aiding the memory

©User Friendly Resource Enterprises. Copying permitted for purchasing school only.

Activity 12 Construct Your Own Mindmaps

- Construct your own mindmap, using the ideas which follow. Use the instructions in the box and the examples on pages 30 and 33 to help you. (Note how each example is different, and very personal to the creator.)

Mindmaps—General Instructions

1) Start with a PICTURE or KEY WORD in the centre of the page.

 Why a Picture?   - It sparks the imagination.
 - It is good to look at.
 - It provides a focus to the topic.

2) From the centre develop BRANCHES for different headings or sub-topics. Use smaller branches to connect ideas together.

3) Use your IMAGINATION to create pictures and symbols.

4) PRINT — using SINGLE KEY WORDS where possible.

5) Use SYMBOLS and SHAPES in creating your Mindmap.

6) In printing and in pictures use BOLD COLOUR to highlight important points.

7) Vary the SIZE of letters and words for effect.

8) Enclose main branches in BALLOONS to keep items together.

9) REARRANGE words or items; eliminate if irrelevant. Some words or ideas could become central pictures themselves.

10) If the Mindmap is to be kept, REDRAW to make it tidy.

Note: Although the Mindmap models are full of colour and pictures, don't worry if you can't draw, or even if you prefer not to have any pictures in your map at all. The beauty about a Mindmap is that is it whatever you want it to be—and it is personal to you.

©User Friendly Resource Enterprises. Copying permitted for purchasing school only.

Setting Your Sights

Mindmap of a hockey coach's team talk.

Note how in this mindmap there are no pictures. The coach used the key words as a summary of his talk.

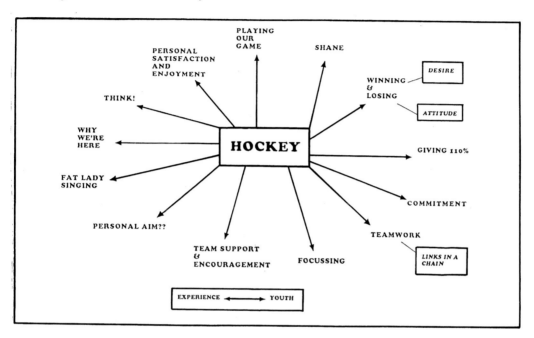

Mindmap for a speech on sailing.

Note the large arrows, which indicate the different aspects of sailing the speaker will develop.

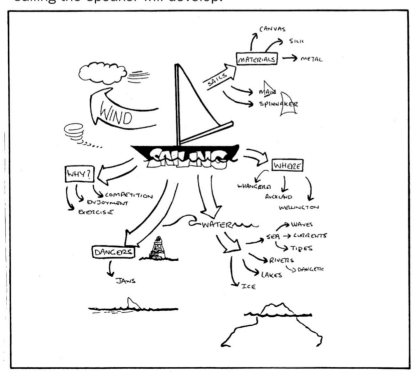

©User Friendly Resource Enterprises. Copying permitted for purchasing school only.

Mindmap 1: Speech on Apples

a) You are asked to give a speech on Apples. Follow the procedure in steps b) to e).

b) Try writing out the speech in longhand. Give yourself 5 minutes, and see how far you get.

c) Brainstorm—with a parent or friend if possible. Write down as many words as you can that may be relevant to the topic. Take another 5 minutes.

d) Organise and put these words into categories. This can be done quickly.

e) Create a mindmap on Apples, using the techniques discussed and illustrated above.

f) Use your mindmap to give your speech to a friend.

Mindmap 2: Brainstorm on Nuclear Testing

a) Use the words you collected in Activity 16, page 41 of Book A, as the basis for making a mindmap on the subject.

b) Remember that the first task is to put the words into groups or categories.

c) Now develop branches from the central title or picture, and add illustrations and other mindmap suggestions to create a visual image of the topic.

Mindmap 3: Novel or Play

a) Take a novel or play you have been studying.

b) Put the title or a picture illustrating the title in the centre.

c) Decide on the categories you will need to use, such as Characters, Setting, Theme and Plot. You should be able to develop a basic mindmap in a very short time.

d) Remember two other advantages of mindmaps as you plan:
- You can link relationships (e.g. between characters) by using arrows and symbols.
- You can add more branches to a main branch at any time. If you are writing an essay it is very difficult to add extra thoughts to a paragraph already written. With a Mindmap, just add another branch.

34

©User Friendly Resource Enterprises. Copying permitted for purchasing school only.

Setting Your Sights

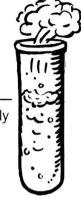

Mindmap 4: Science Experiment

a) Take a science experiment you have been involved in personally or have had demonstrated to you.

b) Decide on what categories you will need in order to create a Mindmap on the subject.

c) Prepare your mindmap.

Mindmap 5: Recent Essay Topic

a) Take an essay topic you have recently been given, and plan it as a mindmap.

b) As you plan, consider each branch as a new paragraph.

c) Now write your essay.

You may find that the mindmap is particularly helpful in organising the order of items in each paragraph.

Mindmap 6: Ten Minute Mindmap

a) Give yourself 10 minutes maximum to create a mindmap on Tourism in France.

b) No hints here—see what you can come up with in a short space of time.

©User Friendly Resource Enterprises. Copying permitted for purchasing school only.

Activity 13 Putting It All Together

- Look at the study ideas below. See how the different intelligences and different learning modes suggest different methods of studying. You probably already use a number of these, but there will be some here that are new to you. Try them!

VISUAL/SPATIAL:
- Draw a chart or diagram.
- Make a Mindmap.
- Draw a poster.
- Create a visual image of your learning—a mental TV documentary.
- Underline or Highlight NEW material.
- Use colour and symbols in your notemaking.

LINGUISTIC:
- Read important sections aloud.
- Use a tape recorder.
- Explain what you have learned to someone else.
- Get a friend to ask you questions.
- Put information in your own words.
- Turn the information into a speech.

PHYSICAL:
- Make notes on flash cards—then arrange in sequence.
- Move about as you learn.
- Act out information you are learning.
- Describe what you are learning using gestures.
- Turn the information you are learning into a model, experiment or diagram.

MATHEMATICAL/ LOGICAL
- Make a flow chart that expresses the learning in a logical, step by step manner.
- List the main points in sequence.
- Compare, contrast and measure the information.
- Classify the information under headings.
- Use prediction—ask "what if" questions.

MUSICAL:
- Use music to get into a relaxed state.
- Create a rhyme and learn this rhythmically.
- Write a song, rap or jingle to summarise your learning.

INTERPERSONAL:
- Work, revise and discuss what you are learning with someone else—"pair and share" as you learn.
- Brainstorm with others.
- Have a group discussion, using appropriate techniques.
- Take different sides of a topic with a friend. Explain each point of view, or debate the topic.

INTRAPERSONAL:
- Think why the subject matters to you. What is its significance to you?
- Take time to reflect quietly on the subject.
- Seek feedback from others and analyse your work methods.
- Think how you can relate the topic to past experience.

36

©User Friendly Resource Enterprises. Copying permitted for purchasing school only.

Activity 14 How Do You Rate As A Listener?

- Read the following story from the Indian philosopher, **Bhagwan Shree Rajneesh**.

> Two men were walking along a crowded street in a busy city. Suddenly one exclaimed, "Listen to the sound of that cricket." But the other could not hear it. He asked his companion how he could hear the sound of the cricket amidst the din of the city traffic. The first man was a zoologist and had trained himself to listen to the voices of nature. He did not explain, but took a coin from his pocket and dropped it on the pavement. Many people stopped and began to look around.
>
> "We hear," he said, "what we listen for."

The point of this story is, that for all sorts of reasons, we rarely **listen carefully enough**. We hear what we expect to hear, or what we want to hear, not what is actually said. In conversations, when supposedly listening, most of us spend time waiting for the chance to speak, preparing what we want to say, instead of actually **listening**.

> Nature has given us one tongue, but two ears, that we may hear from each other twice as much as we speak.
> - **Epictetur**, 1st century Greek philosopher

- So how do you think you rate as a listener? Rate yourself by answering the following questions:

1) Which word best describes you as a listener ?

Superior   Excellent   Above Average   Average   Below Average   Poor

2) Give yourself a mark (0 - 10) as a listener.

- How do you think you would be rated by:

  - your best friend?
  - your parents?
  - your teachers?

©User Friendly Resource Enterprises. Copying permitted for purchasing school only.

3) Is there a difference between these responses and between how you and they rate your listening skills. Why? What do these different responses tell you about your listening skills. Go back to Question 1. Would your rating be different now?

KEYS TO EFFECTIVE LISTENING

1) **Maintain good health**: Make sure your ears are in good shape and healthy, and that you are in overall good physical health.

2) **Concentrate**: If you have difficulty concentrating, say to yourself, "Just for today I am going to make an effort to listen." If you can make today an achieving day, you can do the same tomorrow. Make a commitment to concentrate.

3) **Focus**: Use eye contact and your other senses to help you keep focused on the speaker.

4) **Be active—show interest**: Sit up, look alert, be "all ears"—have an active posture. Have a pen or pencil in your hand, ready to note down key words or ideas as you listen to the speaker.

5) **Give yourself a target**: "I will note down 10 key words in the next 10 minutes as I listen to this talk. There MUST be some useful things here for me."

6) **Listen for clues**: Some examples are, "The first important point ..." or "The crux of the issue is..." or "The key point I want to make is..."

7) **Listen for ideas:** Sort out what the main themes or ideas are in the talk.

8) **Question:** Have a set of How, When, Where, Why, Who, What questions ready. Try to answer these as you listen.

9) **Avoid distractions:** Block out the distracting or clever comments of friends, the restlessness of others, or the game of cricket outside the classroom. Concentrate on the speaker, be focused, be active.

10) **Think respond, challenge**: Your brain can think 4 to 10 times faster than the speed of speech. So while you're listening, use you mental abilities to anticipate, organise, summarise and interpret.

When challenging, it is important to avoid prejudging an argument. The skill is to **listen now, challenge later**.

Stimulate your brain by occasionally listening to more "advanced" or difficult material, or material you would not normally listen to.

11) **Use your imagination:** When listening, create mental images of the words and ideas you are hearing.

©User Friendly Resource Enterprises. Copying permitted for purchasing school only.

Setting Your Sights

Activity 15 Listening Exercises

- Here are some exercises to enhance your listening abilities.

Exercises A and B

Get a parent, teacher or friend to read out to you the listening exercises and questions set out on page 56 of this book. It's important that you don't look at these pages yourself. **After** you've answered the questions, check out the answers below.

ANSWERS

Exercise A: Many people find it hard to give an answer to this question. They say it is not in the story. But listen again, or go to page 54 and read the first word of the first line!

Exercise B: For me, with the name GIFFORD, the line would look like this:

GD _____ GD

Many people will have written the first letter at the beginning and the last letter at the end—like this:

G _____ D

But go back and listen to, or read on page 56, the instructions again.

Exercise C

Go to some different places in your local community—such as the seaside, a bush or forest, a busy city junction, a school playground, a bus stop.

Really listen to the different sounds around you. Isolate machines, wind, birds, feet, high-pitched sounds, low-pitched sounds, different tones of voice and so on.

Maintain silence, and note down and describe all the sounds you can hear. You'll be surprised at the results—and feel quite proud of the list you have compiled.

39

©User Friendly Resource Enterprises. Copying permitted for purchasing school only.

Exercise D

Try this **Effective Listening Quiz**. For each question, tick the category most like you: A = Always; O = Often; S = Seldom; N = Never.

When you take part in a conversation or discussion at school, do you:	A	O	S	N
1. Try to have the last word?				
2. Try to find something useful in what is being said?				
3. Try to judge the value of what has been said, rather than the speaker's ability?				
4. Recognise the difference between fact and opinion?				
5. Try to understand the feelings of the speaker?				
6. Cope with distractions and actively concentrate on listening?				
7. Use body language to show the speaker you are interested?				
8. Enjoy listening to difficult presentations and seminars?				
9. Wait impatiently for the speaker to finish so you can say something?				
10. Finish the sentences of slower speakers yourself?				
11. Establish and maintain eye contact with the speaker?				
12. Interrupt the speaker with clever comments?				
13. Interrupt when you think the speaker has made a mistake?				
14. Put yourself in the speaker's place and try to understand his or her point of view?				

Good listeners will record: An A or O category for questions 2, 3, 4, 5, 6, 7, 8, 11 and 14 and an S or N category for questions 1, 9, 10, 12 and 13.
Remember: There is a difference between hearing and listening.

©User Friendly Resource Enterprises. Copying permitted for purchasing school only.

Effective Reading

Activity 16 Your Reading Speed

• Check your current reading speed by timing yourself, or getting a parent or friend to time you, as you read the extract below. Record the number of seconds you have taken as soon as you finish and complete the calculation that follows the extract.

Under Starter's Orders

For eleven years I roared around the world, but during that time the opportunity to travel on the Trans-Siberian Railway never arose, although I often thought of writing a book about it. Railways, like rivers, are difficult subjects for writers because they go on and on. They are less difficult for writers of fiction who can populate their trains with corpses, villains, beautiful people and wagon-lit attendants with seven o'clock shadow. If they get bored they can blow them up or derail them. A non-fiction writer is lucky if anyone pulls the communication cord.

When the opportunity finally arose I discovered that there were three possibilities open to me. One was simply to apply for a transit visa for the USSR, buy a ticket from Intourist in London and make the journey from Moscow to Nakhodka without getting off the train at all, except to inspire fresh air on the station platforms along the route. An alternative would be to make the journey, stopping over for a day or two at Novosibirsk, Irkutsk, and Khabarovsk, these being the only cities along the route open to foreign visitors in 1977. The third way, and the most complicated and expensive, was to make the journey under the aegis of the Russians themselves and let The Agency provide one of their representatives to accompany me. The Agency is regarded by Western intelligence services as an arm of the KGB. The theoretical advantage of this was that it might be possible to stop off at places that were not on the normal Intourist agenda and see things denied to ordinary foreign tourists, and this was the course I eventually decided upon.

Which was why, in the depths of Arctic January 1977, I found myself keeping a tryst with a senior representative of The Agency in a sauna bath in the West, not much more than a biscuit's toss from the Iron Curtain.

Mr. Oblomov (for that is what I shall call him to spare his blushes), whom I was now regarding through a haze of steam in this subterranean hothouse, was a splendidly endowed fellow in every way, both physically and mentally. Dressed in a Western bespoken suit he had been impressive; now, wearing nothing but a piece of towelling and flagellating himself with a bunch of birch twigs, he looked like a pentathlon gold medallist, and when we plunged into the spacious pool after the torture was over he swam like one.

Later, when I had swum two lengths of the bath under water to show him that, although I was not in the same class as he, I also kept fit, we sat swathed in towels, drinking beer and mapping out a programme for him to present to his superiors.

Two days and three bottles of whisky later - there were others in on this act — I left for London. It had been a thoroughly successful meeting so far as I was concerned. Mr. Oblomov had a list of Siberian Wonders as long as your arm, which if I was able to see only a few of them would have turned me into a Siberian Marco Polo.

It included visits to active volcanoes, to the coldest place in Siberia where temperature descends to -90 degrees F, to the descendants of the Golds, aboriginals, who until comparatively recently had worn suits of skin, to railway construction sites in the remotest wilderness, to gold and

©User Friendly Resource Enterprises. Copying permitted for purchasing school only.

41

diamond mines, ginseng root-collectors and bring-them-back-alive Siberian tiger-hunters. "I shall also," said Mr. Oblomov, "recommend that at least part of your journey should take place while there is still snow on the ground. A visit to Siberia without seeing it under snow is like ..."

"A rose without a thorn?" I suggested.

"I was going to say," he said, mischievously, "like a writer without a head."

The day after I got back to London I received a message to say that I would not be able to make the journey through Siberia with snow on the ground. No reason was given. I suppose they think it makes the place look untidy.

"Your other proposals," the message said, "are being considered." They were still being considered when I caught the train.

(Extract from **The Big Red Train Ride**, Eric Newby, Penguin 1978)

This extract is about 700 words long. To calculate your reading speed in words per minute use this equation:

$$\frac{\text{words} \times 60 \text{ secs}}{\text{secs taken}} = \text{w.p.m.}$$

e.g. $\dfrac{700 \times 60}{60} = 700$ w.p.m.

e.g. $\dfrac{700 \times 60}{180} = 233$ w.p.m.

An "average score" is about 250 w.p.m. Most people can train themselves to increase this by 3, 4, or 5 times, which would enable you to read so much more and be so much more efficient in your reading.

- Without referring to the passage summarise in two or three sentences what it was about.

- Now go to Activities 17 and 18, which give you ideas on developing good reading habits. You'll find that these will help you improve your reading speed...and your comprehension of what you're reading.

42

©User Friendly Resource Enterprises. Copying permitted for purchasing school only.

Activity 17 Developing Good Reading Habits

- Work through the following reading exercises, answering the question that follows each one.

Exercise 1

Time yourself to see how long it takes you to read each of columns A, B, C.

A	B	C
f	forget	Most of the
j	paper	basic gestures
n	sure	are the same
t	end	all over the world.
v	practice	When people are happy
p	each	they smile;
b	secluded	when they are sad
r	calf	or angry
e	gender	they frown or scowl.
z	obese	Nodding the head
k	several	is used
w	jump	to indicate 'yes'.
d	opposite	Shaking the head
q	count	from side to side
a	moist	to indicate 'no'
m	initials	is also universal.

seconds	seconds	seconds
(16 letters)	(16 words)	(49 words)

- What do you notice about these results? Write your answer here.

- -
- -
- -
- -

©User Friendly Resource Enterprises. Copying permitted for purchasing school only.

Exercise 2

Read through this extract:

The President of   General Motors   was in a

foul humour.   He had slept badly   during the night

because his electric blanket   had worked only partly,

causing him to   awaken several times, feeling cold.

to his basement   to repair it.

(Adapted from **Wheels** by Arthur Hailey)

- How are these words arranged? Write your answer here.

- -

- -

- -

Exercise 3

Try to make sense of the extract below. Each __ indicates a missing word. Write in the spaces what you think the missing words might be.

Mike Alexander always __ __ island __ __ own, free __ interfering neighbours. __ __ found __ __ __ Bay __ Islands. __ __ bought Roberton Island 25 years ago __ __ little green cover, __ __ __ spindly scrub __ __ __ half-dozen trees __ __. __ __ started replanting. __ __ now __ green oasis, covered __ regenerating bush. __ __ amazing conservation achievement, he __ __ group __ family __ friends __ restored __ original island cover __ putting __ 60,000 trees, __ natives.

- Now check out your answers to these three exercises with those at the bottom of page 45.

©User Friendly Resource Enterprises. Copying permitted for purchasing school only.

Setting Your Sights

So what's the point of these exercises. The point is that they illustrate a couple of **GOOD READING HABITS**.

1. Read words in **clusters** or **groups**. The eye naturally focuses on a group of words.

2. You don't need to read every word to get meaning from a reading.

Exercise A: Most people find it takes at least as long to read column A as it takes to read column B; and about the same time to read column C, which contains almost three times as many words as in Column B. Obviously, people find it as easy to read groups of words as to read single words.

Exercise B: The words are arranged in **clusters** or **groups**.

Exercise C: Mike Alexander always wanted an island of his own, free from interfering neighbours. And he found it in the Bay of Islands. When he bought Roberton Island 25 years ago it had little green cover, and was mostly spindly scrub with just a half-dozen trees on it. So he started replanting. It is now a green oasis, covered in regenerating bush. In an amazing conservation achievement, he and a group of family and friends have restored the original island cover by putting in 60,000 trees, mostly natives.

(From the **NZ Listener**, 3 May 1997)

©User Friendly Resource Enterprises. Copying permitted for purchasing school only.

Activity 18 Solutions to Common Reading Faults

- Read the following descriptions, noting which ones apply to you. Make a checklist of the suggested remedies for each fault, and pin it up in a place where you'll see it often, such as the noticeboard above your desk at home.

Reading Fault 1: Poor Eye Movements

Just as cricketers and golfers need to keep their heads steady and still when they are hitting the ball, readers need to keep their heads steady and still when reading. Moving one's head about when reading doesn't allow the eyes to focus, and results in slower reading and tired eyes.

Solution: Make use of your peripheral vision (what you see at the edge of your visual range) so that you can keep your head steady as you read. For best peripheral vision hold your book so you can see the whole page (about 40 cm from your eyes).

Reading Fault 2: Mouthing Each Word

This is a habit which can slow down your reading. It takes time to mouth the words and it is unnecessary.

Solution: Keep your mouth closed when reading!

Reading Fault 3: Reading Every Word/One at a Time

Good readers often miss some letters, words (and even phrases) that are of little importance, like of. Slower reading results from reading each word, one word at a time.

Solution: Read words in clusters and groups so that you "glide" over words of little importance. Always moving your eye forward towards the end of each line or on into the next also helps.

Reading Fault 4: Spacing Out

We're all "guilty" of day dreaming and lack of concentration. How often have you come to the end of a page in a book and not had the faintest idea of what you were supposedly reading? This happens to most of us because we lose concentration and are in a spaced-out frame of mind.

©User Friendly Resource Enterprises. Copying permitted for purchasing school only.

Solution: Use the suggestions described in Section 11 of Book C to keep you focused.

Reading Fault 5: Fixation and Regression

This refers to the practice of stopping at difficult words and going back over words. Every time you go back over a word when you're reading, you not only slow yourself down, but you also also tend to lose the pattern of what you are reading. Sometimes it is important to check on the meaning of words, but it is not necessary to do this every time you come across an unfamiliar word. You will often understand the meaning of a word because of its **context**.

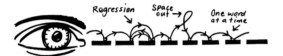

A good reader reads groups of words

Solution: One way to keep you on the ball is to use an appropriate **guide** as you read—a pencil or pen is generally helpful (see also the next point).

Reading Fault 6: Reading Too Slowly

Some people read slowly because they read just one word at a time. However, this method of "uncovering" words one by one is slow and frustrating. Readers have difficulty getting the sense of the extract because they are not using their peripheral vision to move their eyes ahead of the word they are actually reading.

Solution: Recent studies have shown that the use of a guide may increase reading speed by as much as 100%, while also improving your comprehension, understanding and memory. The guide focuses attention, encourages the eye to keep moving in a smooth and rhythmical fashion, and discourages the bad habits of regression, space out and fixation.

The method of guiding that you use is a personal preference. One effective way is to point the guide just beneath the words you are reading. Other people often use a guide running down the middle of the text, or down the side of a page. Another method is to use the "page sweep" technique, where you move your hand in a pattern over the page as you speed read what it contains.

©User Friendly Resource Enterprises. Copying permitted for purchasing school only.

Reading Fault 7: Limited Vocabulary

The more limited your vocabulary, the more difficult it is to read.

Solution: The best way to learn new vocabulary is to practise using new words when you hear them or read them. Bring them into your own speaking and writing. Read widely, read challenging books, and have a dictionary handy when reading. These tactics all assist in developing a stronger vocabulary. Many word games and crossword puzzles are also beneficial in increasing your vocabulary.

©User Friendly Resource Enterprises. Copying permitted for purchasing school only.

Setting Your Sights

Activity 19   Reading With Understanding

- This activity provides several exercises that you can do to help you understand the following points on how to improve your reading comprehension (and speed). Do each exercise in the order given.

1) Check

Ask yourself, why am I reading this? Is it:

    ... to learn it?
    ... to find out what happens next?
    ... to obtain information?
    ... to refresh my memory, revise the material?
    ... to evaluate?
    ... to make notes from it?
    ... to understand the storyline?
    ... to answer a question?
    ... to obtain concrete facts and figures?
    ... to get a different viewpoint on a topic?
    ... for personal enjoyment, relaxation or enrichment?

Your reason for reading the book or article will determine how you approach the reading. Be flexible, and adjust the speed to your need. Some researchers suggest thinking in terms of clothing. You choose what you wear according to the conditions—the weather, the formality of the occasion, your mood. Similarly, you choose a reading style and speed to suit the conditions—what you need to get out of the reading.

So, if you are looking for a particular name or point in a text, you don't have to read the whole book or article. If, on the other hand, you are researching for an essay, you'll need to be reading more slowly and carefully.

2) Scan the Material

When tackling a new book, or even reading an article, the first essential is to **scan**— as you do do when you read a newspaper. On a Saturday morning, your local newspaper probably contains as many words as about five novels. Yet most people read what they want to in about 20 to 40 minutes. How do they do it? By using the main headlines and classified advertising headings to pinpoint what interests them. They read as much or as little as they like.

©User Friendly Resource Enterprises. Copying permitted for purchasing school only.

Similarly, in a book we check the cover, introduction, chapter titles, headings, summaries, pictures, captions, charts, appendices and conclusions.

3) Skim the Material

When you have scanned the whole text, article or book, you will have some idea of where the gold nuggets are. Now skim the text. Slow–skim the parts that scanning has already indicated might be important. Fast–skim or glide over the padding. If you're looking for the answer to a particular question, skim until you reach the relevant section that is likely to contain the answer.

4) Use the First and Last Technique

A good writer will place the main point of a paragraph in the first or last sentence of the paragraph. Similarly, you will often find the main ideas of a chapter summarised in the first and last paragraphs of that chapter. So:

> Read the first and last paragraphs of a chapter.
> Read the first and last sentences of a paragraph.

- At this point, put these ideas into practice by doing the following reading exercises.

EXERCISE A

Underline the <u>key sentences</u> in the following extract. Where do these key sentences appear?

> Property renovating can be a lot of fun and very profitable, but a few simple rules need to be observed. Firstly only consider areas where houses are in good demand. The worst house in the best street is a classic example. It would be a relatively simple and inexpensive matter to renovate that house to a standard equal to those around it. The second rule is to budget on how much you are going to spend on improvements. It is easy to spend too much so be guided by the 3 to 1 rule. That is, every $1 spent on improvements should increase the property resale value by $3.
>
> Follow these simple rules and you can make money in property renovation.

©User Friendly Resource Enterprises. Copying permitted for purchasing school only.

Setting Your Sights

EXERCISE B

What is the **main idea** in the following paragraph?

> Your ear is like the most remarkable musical instrument ever devised. It enables your brain to duplicate the sound of every other instrument, can replay entire symphonies, select and reject sounds at will, and communicate all of this perfectly to your brain. Your ear can discriminate between millions of different nuances of sound. Between the outer layer of the eardrum and your receiving brain there are 10s of 1000s of interdependent structures forming the complete unit.
> (From **Make the Most of your Mind**, Tony Buzan, Pan 1978)

Answer:

....

EXERCISE C

> a) Question: What is it that makes monkeys perform better ?
>
> The programme to train Capuchin monkeys began at Tufts' New England Medical Centre in Boston, Massachusetts. The monkeys here have learned to lock doors, turn lights on and off, bring food from the refrigerator and pick up pencils from the floor. They can push control buttons on self service elevators and pick up a book and put it in someone's hands. After performing a job, the monkeys like to be cuddled and played with. They love attention and work much better when they receive affection.

Answer:

....

51

©User Friendly Resource Enterprises. Copying permitted for purchasing school only.

b) Question: Why do many people have problems with their feet?

Today many people try to fit their feet, which are somewhat flexible, into poorly-shaped shoes for the sake of fashion. Thus many people sooner or later in their lives have problems which stem from ill-fitting shoes. These problems may be direct, such as corns, callouses, bunions or blisters, or they may be indirect, such as a sore back. The only remedy for such problems is to buy shoes which are shaped more like the human foot. Such shoes may look less fashionable, but they are certainly more comfortable.

Answer:

....

5) Use a Guide

We've already looked at this method under Reading Fault Number 7 on page 48. Use the **guide** method that suits you. Make sure you are a chaser—push yourself to read faster by **chasing** your eyes as you read. The chaser system also prevents you from going back over words and having a fixation on others.

Remember that the technique **not** to use is that of uncovering words one by one as you read. Not only is this method inefficient, but it also prevents your eyes developing peripheral vision.

6) Look for Signposts

Be aware of, and follow the writer's directions. Reading is like driving a car and using a street directory or map. There are plenty of directions and signposts along the way to make the process easier.

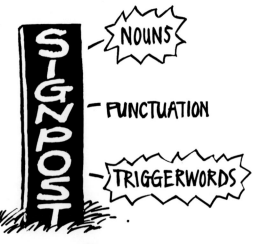

Punctuation is important to gain understanding. Words like in **addition** and **furthermore** alert us that what is about to be said will support the previous sentence. **For example** and for **instance** suggest that the writer is going to support his or her argument with examples and illustrations. The phrase **that is to say** tells you that the writer is about to express his or her thoughts in another way.

©User Friendly Resource Enterprises. Copying permitted for purchasing school only.

Setting Your Sights

EXERCISE D

- Read the following sentence. Then add two commas to the sentence so you completely change its meaning.

> John said Bill was the thief.

- How many meanings can you get from **this** sentence? Try emphasizing each word in turn. Check out your answers with a classmate or friend.

> "I didn't say she hit my dog."

7) Visualisation and Recall

The importance of visualisation has already been emphasised in Section 6. Now is the time to put the visualisation technique into practice when you are reading. When you finish a reading session, ask yourself "What have I been reading about?" Close your eyes and recall it. Try picturing what you have read. This technique can be used in non-fiction articles and in the description of scientific, historical or geographical experiments as well as in literature.

EXERCISE E

Find a recent magazine or newspaper article on a serious topic of about a page in length. Visualise the information, and then recall it—in note form, in a mindmap or by using key words.

8) Be Active in Your Reading

Ask yourself questions. This focuses your mind on what you need to gain from your reading. In particular, can you answer the HWWWWW questions?

9) Note Down Key Points

If it is your own book or article that you are reading, mark key points with a highlighter. To avoid clutter, it is useful to highlight only **new** material. Use your own shorthand in the margin to help when you are reviewing the material (e.g. * = Important; ** = very important; * = needs explanation).

Note down key words, ideas, facts or figures as you read. Use an appropriate notemaking technique—e.g. list the points or use mindmaps. Make your visual and written triggers **bold** and **noticeable**.

©User Friendly Resource Enterprises. Copying permitted for purchasing school only.

10) Extra Hints

* Read one hour per night to develop your reading skills.
* Read aloud—and dramatically. Change your tone, volume, accent.
* Tick lightly (✓) at the end of each paragraph you understand well.
* Have a dictionary handy to check on words (but not every word).
* If you need to go back to a word or section put a * alongside.

©User Friendly Resource Enterprises. Copying permitted for purchasing school only.

Quizzes for Activity 5

Quiz No 1: No Man is An Island

Instructions for the "Quizmaster": This quiz can either be recorded on a tape and played back or read by you as a poem. Tell students to:

Listen to this poem. It is called No Man Is An Island. It consists of 8 lines. As I play (read) the poem try to remember the words. When it finishes, write down as many words as you can remember– in silence.

No Man Is An Island

No man is an Island.
No man stands alone.
Each man's joy is joy to me.
Each man's grief is my own.
We need one another,
So I will defend
Each man as my brother,
Each man as my friend.

Quizmaster: Read through the words again. As you read, ask students to indicate which lines they were able to remember more or less correctly.

Quiz No 2: Word Lists

Instructions for the "Quizmaster": Read the following list of words to students at about 2-second intervals—once only. Tell students to:

Listen to the following set of words. When I have finished reading, write down as many of the words as you can. You must do this in silence.

WORDS

game, sun, real, and, take, steady, rain, saw, and, course, want, ship, recent, and, Shortland Street, plan, some, Queen Elizabeth, keep, and, fine, fresh, fish.

'Quizmaster': Read through the words again. As you read, ask students to indicate which ones they were able to remember.

©User Friendly Resource Enterprises. Copying permitted for purchasing school only.

Listening Exercises For Activity 15

Exercise A

Teacher or parent: Tell students to:

Listen to the story I am about to read to you. When I have finished reading, I will ask you ONE question based on the reading.

Story: You are the Captain of a ship, travelling in a northerly direction off Cape Reinga at a speed of 15 knots. Suddenly, the Captain orders the engine room to change course and to travel at 12 knots in a south-westerly direction for 5 minutes. The Captain then asks the engine room to change direction again and to travel for 10 minutes in an easterly direction at a speed of 11 knots. Finally, the Captain orders the ship to revert to its original speed and direction and to maintain this for 20 minutes.

Question: What is the age of the ship's Captain?

Exercise B

Instructions: Take a piece of paper and draw a horizontal line. Put the first and last letters of your surname at each end of the line you have drawn.

©User Friendly Resource Enterprises. Copying permitted for purchasing school only.